Lament and Love

GW00502165

Lament and Love

The Vision of George Herbert

Compiled by
Robert Van de Weyer and Pat Saunders

LAMP

The Lamp Press
Marshall Morgan and Scott
34—42 Cleveland Street, London W1P 5FB, UK

ISBN 0 551 01827 5

Text Set in Baskerville 10/11pt by Input Typesetting Ltd,
London
Printed in Great Britain by Cox & Wyman Ltd, Reading

Ah my dear angry Lord,
Since thou dost love, yet strike;
Cast down, yet help afford;
Sure I will do the like.
I will complain, yet praise;
I will bewail, approve:
And all my sour-sweet days
I will lament, and love.

.'Bitter-sweet'

Contents

Introduction

For many George Herbert represents all that is fine and good in English spirituality. His poetry is direct and personal, filled with simple, homely images and metaphors; yet it is superbly crafted, with the most subtle rhythms and rhymes. He plumbs the depths of the human spirit, yet he speaks in a language that all can understand, with the minimum of theological argument. In his own life he tried to put into practice what he believed, not by some heroic mission, but by living as a devoted parson in an obscure village. He had a powerful intellect that could have won him great honour in either the academic or political world; yet it was the small, ordinary things of life that excited his keenest interest, and he made even the smallest concerns of his parishioners his own.

Herbert was a child of the English Reformation. Though associated by background and education with the High-Church party within the Anglican Church, his mind and spirit were too broad and supple to be held within any ecclesiastical group. He enjoyed good music, literature, fine clothes, good food; and as a churchman he saw the importance of ritual and sacramental worship. Yet he hankered after simplicity, preferring the quiet rhythm of the countryside to the bustle of London. He also took the spiritual inclinations of country folk as his guide in matters of worship, accepting their distaste for elaborate ceremony and happily maintaining their ancient festivals and customs.

His spirit was nurtured by Cranmer's Book of Common Prayer; and he, and his close friend Nicholas Ferrar, stand out as people who responded to Cranmer's vision for the Church. Until the Reformation, the life of shared daily prayer had been confined to monks and nuns, while lay people, for the most part, merely attended Sunday Mass. But Cranmer condensed the old monastic office into two services, Matins and Evensong, to be the daily worship of the whole Church. Nicholas Ferrar put this into practice in his extended household at Little Gidding: each morning and afternoon the whole community, including families with children, would process from the manor house to their little chapel for prayers. George Herbert, as a country parson, sought to make his parish a praying community: each morning and afternoon he and his family walked from the rectory to the church, inviting other parishioners to share in their worship; and during his brief ministry his parishioners were so warmed by the love and care he showed for them, that many responded. Herbert remains to this day the model which many country clergymen seek to imitate.

Although his ministry as a parson was at Bemerton in Wiltshire, it is the church at Leighton Bromswold in Huntingdonshire that embodies his spirit. Leighton is five miles south of Little Gidding, and when George Herbert became prebend there in 1626 he enlisted the Ferrars' help in restoring the ruined church. It remains to this day virtually as Herbert left it, and contains the finest church furniture of its period in the country; and more particularly its layout shows how Herbert sought to reconcile the Puritan and the High Church attitudes to worship, which were then in such bitter conflict. The visitor is immediately struck by what appear to be two identical pulpits on either side of the chancel arch. In fact the one on the south side is the minister's prayer-desk, and Herbert wished to emphasize that prayer and preaching should have equal importance in public worship – a view that sought to reconcile the Puritan stress on preaching with the High Churchman's emphasis on devotion. In the chancel are benches which appear to be choir stalls, but are, in fact, special pews for communion. Herbert, like the High Churchmen, believed in frequent communion; but, like the Puritans, he preferred to celebrate it with the congregation gathered round the Lord's Table in the chancel, to signify the fellowship between Christians. Thus, in providing benches, rather than forcing the congregation to stand, he enabled a Puritan-style communion to be celebrated in comfort!

George Herbert's writings have an extraordinary capacity to reach across the gulf of four centuries that divides his world from ours, and he seems to penetrate the anguished soul of the late twentieth century. He lived in the formative decades of a culture which is now in decline – a culture which has exalted individual freedom against corporate identity, scientific enquiry against religious faith. Herbert knew, as we are only now beginning to rediscover, that these are false oppositions. The central theme of his poetry is man's interior struggle, the emotional and spiritual conflicts within the individual soul; yet he remains a man of God, knowing that only within the community of God's Church can we find peace and truth. The images in his poems are the everyday objects of life, and even the equipment of the scientist; but he knows that these are merely sacraments of God's presence in the world. Today, after centuries of rampant individualism and indifference to religion, ordinary people are again searching for community, and scientists are beginning to discern divine order in the cosmos. So a poet and a priest who can see the beauty of God within a village dance or a scientific experiment no longer sounds like some deluded madman, but rather a prophet for our time.

* * *

George Herbert was born in 1593 into an old aristocratic family from the Welsh borders. He was only three years old when his father died, so the dominant influence in his childhood years was his mother, Magdalen. She was a devout Christian, and, despite her limited means, entertained lavishly and gave generously to beggars who called in large numbers at her door. She was also a woman of sharp intellect who encouraged the young George Herbert in his studies, and whose ambition for him was always that he should become a priest. When he was twelve she sent him to Westminster School where he came under the influence of the great Dean of the Abbey, Lancelot Andrewes; and in 1609 he won a scholarship to Trinity College, Cambridge.

He was an able scholar, and it was while he was still an undergraduate that he began to write verse, mostly in Latin. On New Year's Day 1609 he sent his mother two Latin sonnets on the theme that the love of God is a fitter subject for verse than the love of women; and, indeed, almost all his poetry was religious. Yet, despite his piety – and relative poverty – George Herbert dressed in expensive clothes, becoming renowned for his elegant appearance, and was also an accomplished musician, playing the lute and composing songs. In 1615 he was elected a fellow of the college, and in 1620 was appointed Public Orator, which was in effect the University's spokesman to the outside world.

Although he still believed he would eventually enter the Church, his role as Public Orator introduced him to Court circles, and political ambitions now took precedence. The Duke of Lennox, King James's closest friend and adviser, became his patron, and George Herbert dreamt of one day becoming Secretary of State. Increasingly he neglected academic work to attend Court, and in 1624 he was elected to Parliament for the old family seat of Montgomery. However, political events were already putting him into a profound moral dilemma which was soon to wreck his career. Princes Charles had been spurned by the King of Spain in his hopes of marrying the Spanish Infanta, and this re-awakened the old rivalry between Spain and England; the Prince himself was trying to gather support for a war against Spain. George Herbert, a peace-lover by conviction and temperament, was horrified, and he decided to use his position as Public Orator to speak out against war. In Prince Charles's presence he delivered a passionate oration, denouncing all those who glorify war, and describing in lurid prose the misery that war causes to ordinary people. Shortly afterwards King James died, and Charles ascended the throne – and George Herbert found himself no longer welcome at court.

The following four years were a time of inward struggle and suffering, and outward uncertainty; and it was during this period that George Herbert wrote almost all his English verse. In 1626 he was ordained deacon, taking the living at Leighton Bromswold in Huntingdonshire. Despite having almost no money of his own, he set his heart on restoring the church, and he persuaded the Duchess of Lennox, who owned the parish, to provide the funds. But he never lived at Leighton, wandering restlessly from one friend's house to another, and paying a curate to care for the parish. In 1627 his mother died, which threw him into even deeper despair. The turning point, however, was when he met and married Jane Danvers, a cousin by marriage, in 1629. She was both beautiful and devout, seemingly without worldly ambition; and it was through the contentment that he found with her that George Herbert finally decided to put aside his own ambitions. At last he felt able to fulfil his mother's original hope for him, to become a country parson – a position held in even lower regard then than now. In 1630 he became rector of Bemerton near Salisbury.

He was already suffering from consumption, and he was to live only another three years; but his ministry at Bemerton continues to inspire the Church of England today. The book which he entitled *The Country Parson* is his description of the ideal rural ministry, and it seems that he came near to fulfilling that ideal himself. Isaak Walton, in his biography of George Herbert, describes how when the bell tolled for Matins and Evensong each day, and George and Jane with their household walked across to the church, even the farm labourers would stop work for a moment to say a prayer. This may seem farfetched, but George Herbert's radiant holiness shining from the pages of *The Country Parson* makes it believable.

George Herbert died on 1 March 1633. A few days earlier he had sent Nicholas Ferrar a manuscript containing his English verses, entitled *The Temple*, asking him to publish or destroy them as he thought fit. Nicholas Ferrar saw clearly the sublime quality of the work, and decided it should be published. There was some delay in getting the book licensed for publication since the Vice-Chancellor of Cambridge University wanted to delete the controversial couplet:

> Religion stands on tiptoe in our land
> Ready to pass to the American strand.

But Ferrar refused to tamper with the text, and eventually it was printed in its original form. It was an extraordinary success, selling over twenty-thousand copies within the next thirty years. Herbert in his lifetime had retired into obscurity; but Herbert after his death was recognized as one of the finest poets of the English Church, and also one of her saints.

* * *

Nicholas Ferrar in his introduction to *The Temple* wrote:

'The dedication of this work having been made by the author to the divine majesty only, how shall we now presume to interest any mortal man in the patronage of it? Much less think we it meet to seek the recommendation of the Muses, for that which himself was confident to have been inspired by a diviner breath than flows from helicon. The world therefore shall receive it in that naked simplicity, with which he left it, without any addition either of support or ornament, more than is included in itself.'

In his English poems George Herbert laid bare his soul: he himself says that we are to find in them 'a picture of the many spiritual conflicts that have passed betwixt God and my soul, before I could subject mine to the will of Jesus, my Master'. Reading the poems one often feels one is intruding in a private conversation between an individual and his Maker, and one can even be shocked at the poet's frankness, and his rejection of any kind of conventional piety to disguise his personal struggle. The poems have the same brutal honesty as the Psalms, in which every emotion and feeling – good or bad, loving or hateful – is offered to God. Yet, although they are intimate in content, in style and execution they are the work of a master craftsman whose poetic skill bears comparison with that of Shakespeare. As one reads and rereads each poem one is enthralled by the agility and the variety of his metres and rhymes, by the juxtaposition of familiar images to create fresh pictures in one's mind, and even by the shape of the verses on the page – indeed in some poems, such as Easter Wings, the shape deliberately illustrates the subject.

Although the poems were composed over several years, George Herbert himself decided the sequence in which they should appear in *The Temple*; and critics have debated long and hard over what meaning should be attached to their order. Any selection of the poems must, however, break that original order; and in our selection the poems are arranged under themes. It is not a purely personal selection – others, like R. S. Thomas and W. H. Auden, have published their own choice of Herbert's poetry – but is an attempt to give a rounded picture of the themes, subjects and styles of his work. But, of course, each poem stands on its own, and they should be read and enjoyed individually.

The Country Parson has the same intimacy and richness of expression as the poetry, but is concerned with the outward, practical application of Christian devotion. It can be read as a simple guide as to how the parson should perform his job. But it is also a beautiful, sublime description of the life of a saint, living amongst ordinary village folk. One can see the cottages and the muddy street of the village, one can hear the voices of the labourers, and even smell the livestock; at one end of the village one imagines the church, clean and plain, the rectory with its simple, sturdy furniture, and the rectory garden filled with flowers and medicinal herbs; and, of course, there is George Herbert in his sober apparel visiting the sick and elderly, chatting amiably to the farmers and craftsmen, and walking with Jane each morning and afternoon to church for the daily office. As any country parson will affirm, it is a book filled with wise advice and pastoral insight; and we hope our choice of passages shows that it is as relevant today as it was in the seventeenth century.

Amongst the manuscripts found after George Herbert's death was his collection of Outlandish Proverbs. These are both witty and wise, enjoyable for their own sake, and valuable as further insight into the mind of the man who thought them worth recording. Some are also to be found amongst the manuscripts of the Little Gidding Community, which suggests that George Herbert and the Ferrar family shared this pleasurable hobby. There are over a thousand proverbs in the original collection, of which only a selection are included here, arranged according to their subject.

The final piece in the present volume is an extract from the speech which cost George Herbert his political career. It was delivered in October 1623, and it ranks alongside the speeches made in our own time by Gandhi and Martin Luther King in the cause of peace. The original text is in Latin, so this extract is a translation.

POETRY

Festivals

Christmas

All after pleasures as I rid one day,
  My horse and I, both tir'd, body and mind,
  With full cry of affections, quite astray;
I took up in the next inn I could find.

There when I came, whom found I but my dear,
  My dearest Lord, expecting till the grief
  Of pleasures brought me to him, ready there
To be all passengers' most sweet relief?

Oh Thou, whose glorious, yet contracted light,
  Wrapt in night's mantle, stole into a manger;
  Since my dark soul and brutish is thy right,
To Man of all beasts be not thou a stranger:

  Furnish and deck my soul, that thou mayst have
  A better lodging, than a rack, or grave.

Lent

Welcome dear feast of Lent: who loves not thee,
He loves not Temperance, or Authority,
    But is compos'd of passion.
The Scriptures bid us *fast*; the Church says, *now*:
Give to thy Mother, what thou wouldst allow
    To ev'ry Corporation.

Besides the cleanness of sweet abstinence,
Quick thoughts and motions at a small expense,
      A face not fearing light:
Whereas in fullness there are sluttish fumes,
Sour exhalations, and dishonest rheums,
      Revenging the delight.

Then those same pendant profits, which the spring
And Easter intimate, enlarge the thing,
      And goodness of the deed.
Neither ought other men's abuse of Lent
Spoil the good use; lest by that argument
      We forfeit all our Creed.

It's true, we cannot reach Christ's forti'th day;
Yet to go part of that religious way,
      Is better than to rest:
We cannot reach our Saviour's purity;
Yet are we bid, *Be holy ev'n as he.*
      In both let's do our best.

Who goeth in the way which Christ hath gone,
Is much more sure to meet with him, than one
      That travelleth byways:
Perhaps my God, though he be far before,
May turn, and take me by the hand, and more
      May strengthen my decays.

Yet Lord instruct us to improve our fast
By starving sin and taking such repast,
      As may our faults control:
That ev'ry man may revel at his door,
Not in his parlour; banqueting the poor,
      And among those his soul.

Good Friday

Oh my chief good,
How shall I measure out thy blood?
How shall I count what thee befell,
    And each grief tell?

Shall I thy woes
Number according to thy foes?
Or, since one star show'd thy first breath,
    Shall all thy death?

Or shall each leaf,
Which falls in Autumn, score a grief?
Or cannot leaves, but fruit, be sign
    Of the true vine?

Then let each hour
Of my whole life one grief devour;
That thy distress through all may run,
    And be my sun.

Or rather let
My several sins their sorrows get;
That as each beast his cure doth know,
    Each sin may so.

Redemption

Having been tenant long to a rich Lord,
   Not thriving, I resolved to be bold,
   And make a suit unto him, to afford
A new small-rented lease, and cancel th' old.

In heaven at his manor I him sought:
   They told me there, that he was lately gone
   About some land, which he had dearly bought
Long since on earth, to take possession.

I straight return'd, and knowing his great birth,
   Sought him accordingly in great resorts;
   In cities, theatres, gardens, parks, and courts:
At length I heard a ragged noise and mirth

   Of thieves and murderers: there I him espied,
   Who straight, *Your suit is granted* said, and died.

Sepulchre

Oh blessed body! Whither art thou thrown?
No lodging for thee, but a cold hard stone?
So many hearts on earth, and yet not one
         Receive thee?

Sure there is room within our hearts' good store;
For they can lodge transgressions by the score:
Thousands of toys dwell there, yet out of door
         They leave thee.

But that which shows them large, shows them unfit.
Whatever sin did this pure rock commit,
Which holds thee now? Who hath indicted it
         Of murder?

Where our hard hearts have took up stones to brain thee,
And missing this, most falsely did arraign thee;
Only these stones in quiet entertain thee,
         And order.

And as of old, the law by heav'nly art
Was writ in stone; so thou, which also art
The letter of the word, find'st no fit heart
         To hold thee.

Yet do we still persist as we began,
And so should perish, but that nothing can,
Though it be cold, hard, foul, from loving man
         Withold thee.

Easter Wings

Lord, who createdst man in wealth and store,
    Though foolishly he lost the same,
        Decaying more and more,
           Till he became
             Most poor:
             With thee
           Oh let me rise
        As larks, harmoniously,
    And sing this day thy victories:
Then shall the fall further the flight in me.

My tender age in sorrow did begin:
    And still with sicknesses and shame
        Thou didst so punish sin,
           That I became
             Most thin.
             With thee
           Let me combine,
        And feel this day thy victory:
    For, if I imp my wing on thine,
Affliction shall advance the flight in me.

Whitsunday

Listen sweet Dove unto my song,
    And spread thy golden wings in me;
    Hatching my tender heart so long,
Till it get wing, and fly away with thee.

Where is that fire which once descended
    On thy Apostles? thou didst then
    Keep open house, richly attended,
Feasting all comers by twelve chosen men.

But since those pipes of gold, which brought
    That cordial water to our ground,

Were cut and martyr'd by the fault
Of those, who did themselves through their side wound,

Thou shutt'st the door, and keep'st within;
Scarce a good joy creeps through the chink:
And if the braves of conqu'ring sin
Did not excite thee, we should wholly sink.

Lord, though we change, thou art the same;
The same sweet God of love and light:
Restore this day, for thy great name,
Unto his ancient and miraculous right.

Trinity Sunday

Lord, who hast form'd me out of mud,
And hast redeem'd me through thy blood,
And sanctifi'd me to do good;

Purge all my sins done heretofore:
For I confess my heavy score,
And I will strive to sin no more.

Enrich my heart, mouth, hands in me,
With faith, with hope, with charity;
That I may run, rise, rest with thee.

Church Worship

Antiphon

Choir. Let all the world in ev'ry corner sing,
  My God and King.

Verse. The heav'ns are not too high,
　　His praise may thither fly:
　　The earth is not too low,
　　His praises there may grow.

Choir. Let all the world in ev'ry corner sing,
　　My God and King.

Verse. The church with psalms must shout,
　　No door can keep them out:
　　But above all, the heart
　　Must bear the longest part.

Choir. Let all the world in ev'ry corner sing,
　　My God and King.

Matins

　　I cannot ope mine eyes,
　But thou art ready there to catch
　My morning soul and sacrifice:
Then we must needs for that day make a match.

　　My God, what is a heart?
　Silver, or gold, or precious stone,
　Or star, or rainbow, or a part
Of all these things, or all of them in one?

　　My God, what is a heart,
　That thou shouldst it so eye, and woo,
　Pouring upon it all thy art,
As if that thou hadst nothing else to do?

　　Indeed man's whole estate
　Amounts (and richly) to serve thee:
　He did not heav'n and earth create,
Yet studies them, not him by whom they be.

17

Teach me thy love to know;
That this new light, which now I see,
May both the work and workman show:
Then by a sunbeam I will climb to thee.

Evensong

Blest be the God of love,
Who gave me eyes, and light, and power this day,
  Both to be busy, and to play.
  But much more blest be God above,
    Who gave me sight alone,
    Which to himself he did deny:
  For when he sees my ways, I die:
But I have got his son, and he hath none.

What have I brought thee home
For this thy love? have I discharg'd the debt,
  Which this day's favour did beget?
  I ran; but all I brought, was foam.
    Thy diet, care, and cost
    Do end in bubbles, balls of wind;
  Of wind to thee whom I have crost,
But balls of wildfire to my troubled mind.

Yet still thou goest on,
And now with darkness closest weary eyes,
  Saying to man, *It doth suffice:*
  Henceforth repose; your work is done.
    Thus in thy Ebony box
    Thou dost enclose us, till the day
  Put our amendment in our way,
And give new wheels to our disorder'd clocks.

I muse, which shows more love,
The day or night: that is the gale, this th' harbour;
  That is the walk, and this the arbour;
  Or that the garden, this the grove.

My God, thou art all love.
Not one poor minute scapes thy breast,
But brings a favour from above;
And in this love, more than in bed, I rest.

Sunday

Oh day most calm, most bright,
The fruit of this, the next world's bud,
Th' endorsement of supreme delight,
Writ by a friend, and with his blood;
The couch of time; care's balm and bay:
The week were dark, but for thy light:
    Thy torch doth show the way.

The other days and thou
Make up one man; whose face thou art,
Knocking at heaven with thy brow:
The worky-days are the back-part;
The burden of the week lies there,
Making the whole to stoop and bow,
    Till thy release appear.

Man had straight forward gone
To endless death: but thou dost pull
And turn us round to look on one,
Whom, if we were not very dull,
We could not choose but look on still;
Since there is no place so alone,
    The which he doth not fill.

Sundays the pillars are,
On which heav'n's palace arched lies:
The other days fill up the spare
And hollow room with vanities.
They are the fruitful beds and borders
In God's rich garden: that is bare,
    Which parts their ranks and orders.

The Sundays of man's life,
Threaded together on time's string,
Make bracelets to adorn the wife
Of the eternal glorious King.
On Sunday heaven's gate stands ope;
Blessings are plentiful and rife,
 More plentiful than hope.

 This day my Saviour rose,
And did enclose this light for his:
That, as each beast his manger knows,
Man might not of his fodder miss.
Christ hath took in this piece of ground,
And made a garden there for those
 Who want herbs for their wound.

 The rest of our Creation
Our great Redeemer did remove
With the same shake, which at his passion
Did th' earth and all things with it move.
As Samson bore the doors away,
Christ's hands, though nail'd, wrought our salvation,
 And did unhinge that day.

 The brightness of that day
We sullied by our foul offence:
Wherefore that robe we cast away,
Having a new at his expense,
Whose drops of blood paid the full price,
That was requir'd to make us gay,
 And fit for Paradise.

 Thou art a day of mirth:
And where the weekdays trail on ground,
Thy flight is higher, as thy birth.
Oh let me take thee at the bound,
Leaping with thee from sev'n to sev'n,
Till that we both, being toss'd from earth,
 Fly hand in hand to heav'n!

The Holy Communion

Not in rich furniture, or fine array,
    Nor in a wedge of gold,
    Thou, who from me wast sold,
  To me dost now thyself convey;
For so thou should'st without me still have been,
    Leaving within me sin:

But by the way of nourishment and strength
    Thou creep'st into my breast;
    Making thy way my rest,
  And thy small quantities my length;
Which spread their forces into every part,
    Meeting sin's force and art.

Yet can these not get over to my soul,
    Leaping the wall that parts
    Our souls and fleshly hearts;
  But as th' outworks, they may control
My rebel flesh, and carrying thy name,
    Affright both sin and shame.

Only thy grace, which with these elements comes,
    Knoweth the ready way,
    And hath the privy key,
  Op'ning the soul's most subtle rooms;
While those to spirits refin'd, at door attend
    Dispatches from their friend.

Holy Baptism

    Since, Lord, to thee
  A narrow way and little gate
Is all the passage, on my infancy
  Thou didst lay hold, and antedate
    My faith in me.

> Oh let me still
>   Write thee great God, and me a child:
> Let me be soft and supple to thy will,
>   Small to myself, to others mild,
>   Behither ill.

>   Although by stealth
>   My flesh get on; yet let her sister
> My soul bid nothing, but preserve her wealth:
>   The growth of flesh is but a blister;
>   Childhood is health.

Prayer

> Of what an easy quick access,
> My blessed Lord, art thou! how suddenly
>   May our requests thine ear invade!
> To show that state dislikes not easyness,
> If I but lift mine eyes, my suit is made:
> Thou canst no more not hear, than thou canst die.

> Of what supreme almighty power
> Is thy great arm which spans the east and west,
>   And tacks the centre to the sphere!
> By it do all things live their measur'd hour:
> We cannot ask the thing, which is not there,
> Blaming the shallowness of our request.

> Of what unmeasurable love
> Art thou possest, who, when thou couldst not die,
>   Wert fain to take our flesh and curse,
> And for our sakes in person sin reprove,
> That by destroying that which tied thy purse,
> Thou mightst make sure for liberality!

> Since then these three wait on thy throne,
> *Ease, Power,* and *Love*; I value prayer so,
>   That were I to leave all but one,

Wealth, fame, endowments, virtues, all should go;
I and dear prayer would together dwell,
And quickly gain, for each inch lost, an ell.

Praise

King of Glory, King of Peace,
      I will love thee:
And that love may never cease,
      I will move thee.

Thou has granted my request,
      Thou hast heard me:
Thou didst note my working breast,
      Thou hast spar'd me.

Wherefore with my utmost art
      I will sing thee,
And the cream of all my heart
      I will bring thee.

Though my sins against me cried,
      Thou didst clear me;
And alone, when they replied,
      Thou didst hear me.

Sev'n whole days, not one in seven,
      I will praise thee.
In my heart, though not in heaven,
      I can raise thee.

Thou grew'st soft and moist with tears,
      Thou relentedst:
And when Justice call'd for fears,
      Thou dissentedst.

Small it is, in this poor sort
      To enroll thee:

Ev'n eternity is too short
　　To extol thee.

The Church Building

The Church Porch

Avoid profaneness; come not here:
Nothing but holy, pure, and clear,
Or that which groaneth to be so,
May at his peril further go.

Church Lock and Key

I know it is my sin, which locks thine ears,
　　And binds thy hands,
Outcrying my requests, drowning my tears;
Or else the chillness of my faint demands.

But as cold hands are angry with the fire,
　　And mend it still;
So I do lay the want of my desire,
Not on my sins, or coldness, but thy will.

Yet hear, Oh God, only for his blood's sake
　　Which pleads for me:
For though sins plead too, yet like stones they make
His blood's sweet current much more loud to be.

24

The Church Floor

Mark you the floor? that square and speckled stone,
    Which looks so firm and strong,
        Is *Patience*:

And th' other black and grave, wherewith each one
    Is checker'd all along,
        Humility:

The gentle rising, which on either hand
    Leads to the Choir above,
        Is *Confidence*:

But the sweet cement, which in one sure band
    Ties the whole frame, is *Love*
        And *Charity*

    Hither sometimes Sin steals, and stains
    The marble's neat and curious veins:
But all is cleansed when the marble weeps.
    Sometimes Death, puffing at the door,
    Blows all the dust about the floor:
But while he thinks to spoil the room, he sweeps.
    Blest be the *Architect*, whose art
    Could build so strong in a weak heart.

The Windows

Lord, how can man preach thy eternal word?
    He is a brittle crazy glass:
Yet in thy temple thou dost him afford
    This glorious and transcendent place,
    To be a window, through thy grace.

But when thou dost anneal in glass thy story,
    Making thy life to shine within
The holy Preacher's; then the light and glory

More rev'rend grows, and more doth win:
Which else shows wat'rish, bleak, and thin.

Doctrine and life, colours and light, in one
    When they combine and mingle, bring
A strong regard and awe: but speech alone
    Doth vanish like a flaring thing,
    And in the ear, not conscience ring.

The Altar

A broken A L T A R, Lord, thy servant rears,
Made of a heart, and cemented with tears:
    Whose parts are as thy hand did frame;
    No workman's tool hath touch'd the same.
          A H E A R T alone
          Is   such   a   stone,
          As   nothing   but
          Thy pow'r doth cut.
          Wherefore each part
          Of my hard heart
          Meets in this frame,
          To praise thy name.
  That if I chance to hold my peace,
  These stones to praise thee may not cease.
Oh let thy blessed S A C R I F I C E be mine,
And sanctify this A L T A R to be thine.

Church Monuments

While that my soul repairs to her devotion,
Here I entomb my flesh, that it betimes
May take acquaintance of this heap of dust;
To which the blast of death's incessant motion,
Fed with the exhalation of our crimes,
Drive all at last. Therefore I gladly trust

My body to this school, that it may learn
To spell his elements, and find his birth
Written in dusty heraldry and lines;
Which dissolution sure doth best discern,
Comparing dust with dust, and earth with earth.
These laugh at Jet, and Marble put for signs,

To sever the good fellowship of dust,
And spoil the meeting. What shall point out them,
When they shall bow, and kneel, and fall down flat
To kiss those heaps, which now they have in trust?
Dear flesh, while I do pray, learn here thy stem
And true descent; that when thou shalt grow fat,

And wanton in thy cravings, thou mayst know,
That flesh is but the glass, which holds the dust
That measures all our time; which also shall
Be crumbled into dust. Mark here below
How tame these ashes are, how free from lust,
That thou mayst fit thy self against thy fall.

The Cross

What is this strange and uncouth thing?
To make me sigh, and seek, and faint, and die,
Until I had some place, where I might sing,
        And serve thee; and not only I,
But all my wealth and family might combine
To set thy honour up, as our design.

And then when after much delay,
Much wrestling, many a combat, this dear end,
So much desir'd, is giv'n, to take away
        My power to serve thee; to unbend
All my abilities, my designs confound,
And lay my threat'nings bleeding on the ground.

One ague dwelleth in my bones,
Another in my soul (the memory
What I would do for thee, if once my groans
    Could be allow'd for harmony)
I am in all a weak disabled thing,
Save in the sight thereof, where strength doth sting.

    Besides, things sort not to my will,
Ev'n when my will doth study thy renown:
Thou turnest th' edge of all things on me still,
    Taking me up to throw me down:
So that, ev'n when my hopes seem to be sped,
I am to grief alive, to them as dead.

    To have my aim, and yet to be
Further from it than when I bent my bow;
To make my hopes my torture, and the fee
    Of all my woes another woe,
Is in the midst of delicates to need,
And ev'n in Paradise to be a weed.

    Ah my dear Father, ease my smart!
These contrarieties crush me: these cross actions
Do wind a rope about, and cut my heart:
    And yet since these thy contradictions
Are properly a cross felt by thy Son,
With but four words, my words, *Thy will be done.*

Church Music

Sweetest of sweets, I thank you: when displeasure
    Did through my body wound my mind,
You took me thence, and in your house of pleasure
    A dainty lodging me assign'd.

Now I in you without a body move,
    Rising and falling with your wings:
We both together sweetly live and love,
    Yet say sometimes, *God help poor Kings.*

Comfort, I'll die; for if you post from me,
    Sure I shall do so, and much more:
But if I travel in your company,
    You know the way to heaven's door.

The Bible

The Holy Scriptures

Oh Book! infinite sweetness! let my heart
    Suck ev'ry letter, and a honey gain,
    Precious for any grief in any part;
To clear the breast, to mollify all pain.

Thou art all health, health thriving till it make
    A full eternity: thou art a mass
    Of strange delights, where we may wish and take.
Ladies, look here; this is the thankful glass,

That mends the looker's eyes; this is the well
    That washes what it shows. Who can endear
    Thy praise too much? thou art heav'ns Lidger here,
Working against the states of death and hell.

    Thou art joy's handsel: heav'n lies flat in thee,
    Subject to ev'ry mounter's bended knee.

The 23rd Psalm

The God of love my shepherd is,
    And he that doth me feed:
While he is mine, and I am his,
    What can I want or need?

He leads me to the tender grass,
   Where I both feed and rest;
Then to the streams that gently pass:
   In both I have the best.

Or if I stray, he doth convert
   And bring my mind in frame:
And all this not for my desert,
   But for his holy name.

Yea, in death's shady black abode
   Well may I walk, not fear:
For thou art with me; and thy rod
   To guide, thy staff to bear.

Nay, thou dost make me sit and dine,
   Ev'n in my enemy's sight:
My head with oil, my cup with wine
   Runs over day and night.

Surely thy sweet and wondrous love
   Shall measure all my days;
And as it never shall remove,
   So neither shall my praise.

The Pearl. Matthew 13:45–46

I know the ways of Learning; both the head
And pipes that feed the press, and make it run;
What reason hath from nature borrowed,
Or of itself, a good huswife, spun
In laws and policy; what the stars conspire,
What willing nature speaks, what forc'd by fire;
Both th' old discoveries, and the new-found seas,
The stock and surplus, cause and history:
All these stand open, or I have the keys:
       Yet I love thee.

I know the ways of Honour, what maintains
The quick returns of courtesy and wit:
In vies of favours whether party gains,
When glory swells the heart, and mouldeth it
To all expressions both of hand and eye,
Which on the world a true-love-knot may tie,
And bear the bundle, whereso'er it goes:
How many drams of spirit there must be
To sell my life unto my friends or foes:
   Yet I love thee.

I know the ways of Pleasure, the sweet strains,
The lullings and the relishes of it;
The propositions of hot blood and brains;
What mirth and music mean; what love and wit
Have done these twenty hundred years, and more:
I know the projects of unbridled store:
My stuff is flesh, not brass; my senses live,
And grumble oft, that they have more in me
Than he that curbs them being but one to five:
   Yet I love thee.

I know all these, and have them in my hand;
Therefore not sealed, but with open eyes
I fly to thee, and fully understand
Both the main sale, and the commodities,
And at what rate and price I have thy love;
With all the circumstances that may move:
Yet through the labyrinths, not my groveling wit,
But thy silk twist let down from heav'n to me.
But both conduct and teach me, how by it
   To climb to thee.

The Odour. 2 Corinthians 2

How sweetly doth *My Master* sound! *My Master!*
 As Ambergris leaves a rich scent
  Unto the taster:

So do these words a sweet content,
An oriental fragrancy, *My Master*.

With these all day I do perfume my mind,
   My mind ev'n thrust into them both:
      That I might find
   What cordials make this curious broth,
This broth of smells, that feeds and fats my mind.

My Master shall I speak? Oh that to thee
   My servant were a little so,
      As flesh may be;
   That these two words might creep and grow
To some degree of spiciness to thee!

Then should the Pomander, which was before
   A speaking sweet, mend by reflection,
      And tell me more:
   For pardon of my imperfection
Would warm and work it sweeter than before.

For when *My Master*, which alone is sweet,
   And ev'n in my unworthiness pleasing,
      Shall call and meet,
   My servant as thee not displeasing,
That call is but the breathing of the sweet.

This breathing would with gains by sweet'ning me
   (As sweet things traffic when they meet)
      Return to thee.
   And so this new commerce and sweet
Should all my life employ, and busy me.

Ephesians 4:30

Grieve not the Holy Spirit

And art thou grieved, sweet and sacred Dove,
      When I am sour,
        And cross thy love?

Grieved for me? the God of strength and power
   Griev'd for a worm, which when I tread,
   I pass away and leave it dead?

Then weep mine eyes, the God of love doth grieve:
      Weep foolish heart,
      And weeping live:
For death is dry as dust. Yet if ye part,
   End as the night, whose sable hue
   Your sins express; melt into dew.

When saucy mirth shall knock or call at door,
      Cry out, Get hence,
      Or cry no more.
Almighty God doth grieve, he puts on sense:
   I sin not to my grief alone,
   But to my God's, too: he doth groan.

Oh take thy lute, and tune it to a strain,
      Which may with thee
      All day complain.
There can no discord but in ceasing be.
   Marbles can weep; and surely strings
   More bowels have, than such hard things.

Lord, I adjudge myself to tears and grief,
      Ev'n endless tears
      Without relief.
If a clear spring for me no time forebears,
   But runs, although I be not dry;
   I am no Crystal, what shall I?

Yet if I wail not still, since still to wail
      Nature denies;
      And flesh would fail,
If my deserts were masters of mine eyes:
   Lord, pardon, for thy son makes good
   My want of tears with store of blood.

Colossians 3:3

Our life is hid with Christ in God

My words and thoughts do both express this notion,
That   *Life* hath with the sun a double motion.
The first   *Is* straight, and our diurnal friend,
The other   *Hid*, and doth obliquely bend.
Our life is wrapt   *In* flesh, and tends to earth.
The other winds towards   *Him*, whose happy birth
Taught me to live here so,   *That* still one eye
Should aim and shoot at that which *Is* on high:
Quitting   with   daily   labour   all   *My* pleasure,
To   gain   at   harvest   an   eternal   *Treasure*.

Mary Magdalene

When blessed Mary wip'd her Saviour's feet,
(Whose precepts she had trampled on before)
And wore them for a jewel on her head,
   Showing his steps should be the street,
   Wherein she thenceforth evermore
With pensive humbleness would live and tread:

She being stain'd herself, why did she strive
To make him clean, who could not be defil'd?
Why kept she not her tears for her own faults,
   And not his feet? Though we could dive
   In tears like seas, our sins are pil'd
Deeper than they, in words, and works, and thoughts.

Dear soul, she knew who did vouchsafe and deign
To bear her filth; and that her sins did dash
Ev'n God himself: wherefore she was not loath,
   As she had brought wherewith to stain,
   So to bring in wherewith to wash:
And yet in washing one, she washed both.

Jesu

JESU is in my heart, his sacred name
Is deeply carved there: but th' other week
A great affliction broke the little frame,
Ev'n all to pieces: which I went to seek:
And first I found the corner, where was *J*,
After, where *ES*, and next where *U* was graved.
When I had got these parcels, instantly
I sat me down to spell them, and perceived
That to my broken heart he was *I ease you*,
       And to my whole is *JESU*.

Christian Life

The Elixir

    Teach me, my God and King,
      In all things thee to see,
And what I do in anything,
      To do it as for thee:

    Not rudely, as a beast,
      To run into an action;
But still to make thee prepossest,
      And give it his perfection.

    A man that looks on glass,
      On it may stay his eye;
Or if he pleaseth, through it pass,
      And then the heav'n espy.

    All may of thee partake:
      Nothing can be so mean,

Which with this tincture (for thy sake)
        Will not grow bright and clean.

    A servant with this clause
    Makes drudgery divine:
Who sweeps a room, as for thy laws,
    Makes that and th' action fine.

    This is the famous stone
    That turneth all to gold:
For that which God doth touch and own
    Cannot for less be told.

Praise

To write a verse or two, is all the praise,
        That I can raise:
    Mend my estate in any ways,
        Thou shalt have more.

I go to Church; help me to wings, and I
        Will thither fly;
    Or, if I mount unto the sky,
        I will do more.

Man is all weakness, there is no such thing
        As Prince or King:
    His arm is short; yet with a sling
        He may do more.

An herb distill'd, and drunk, may dwell next door,
        On the same floor,
    To a brave soul: Exalt the poor,
        They can do more.

Oh raise me then! Poor bees, that work all day,
        Sting my delay,
    Who have a work, as well as they,
        And much, much more.

Content

Peace mutt'ring thoughts, and do not grudge to keep
    Within the walls of your own breast:
Who cannot on his own bed sweetly sleep,
    Can on another's hardly rest.

Gad not abroad at ev'ry quest and call
    Of an untrained hope or passion.
To court each place or fortune that doth fall,
    Is wantonness in contemplation.

Mark how the fire in flints doth quiet lie,
    Content and warm t' itself alone:
But when it would appear to other's eye,
    Without a knock it never shone.

Give me the pliant mind, whose gentle measure
    Complies and suits with all estates;
Which can let loose to a crown, and yet with pleasure
    Take up within a cloister's gates.

This soul doth span the world, and hang content
    From either pole unto the centre:
Wherein each room of the well-furnish'd tent
    He lies warm, and without adventure.

The brags of life are but a nine days' wonder;
    And after death the fumes that spring
From private bodies, make as big a thunder,
    As those which rise from a huge King.

Only thy Chronicle is lost; and yet
    Better by worms be all once spent,
Than to have hellish moths still gnaw and fret
    Thy name in books, which may not rent:

When all thy deeds, whose brunt thou feel'st alone,
    Are chaw'd by others' pens and tongue;

And as their wit is, their digestion,
    Thy nourish'd fame is weak or strong.

Then cease discoursing soul, till thine own ground,
    Do not thyself or friends importune.
He that by seeking hath himself once found,
    Hath ever found a happy fortune.

Hope

I gave to Hope a watch of mine: but he
    An anchor gave to me.
Then an old prayer book I did present:
    And he an optic sent.
With that I gave a vial full of tears:
    But he a few green ears:
Ah Loiterer! I'll no more, no more I'll bring:
    I did expect a ring.

Grace

My stock lies dead, and no increase
Doth my dull husbandry improve:
Oh let thy graces without cease
    Drop from above!

If still the sun should hide his face,
Thy house would but a dungeon prove,
Thy works night's captives: Oh let grace
    Drop from above!

The dew doth ev'ry morning fall;
And shall the dew outstrip thy Dove?
The dew, for which grass cannot call,
    Drop from above.

Death is still working like a mole,

And digs my grave at each remove:
Let grace work too, and on my soul
Drop from above.

Sin is still hammering my heart
Unto a hardness, void of love:
Let suppl'ing grace, to cross his art,
Drop from above.

Oh come! for thou dost know the way.
Or if to me thou wilt not move,
Remove me, where I need not say.
Drop from above.

Gratefulness

Thou that hast giv'n so much to me,
Give one thing more, a grateful heart.
See how thy beggar works on thee
By art.

He makes thy gifts occasion more,
And says, If he in this be cross'd,
All thou hast giv'n him heretofore
Is lost.

But thou didst reckon, when at first
Thy word our hearts and hands did crave,
What it would come to at the worst
To save.

Perpetual knockings at thy door,
Tears sullying thy transparent rooms,
Gift upon gift, much would have more,
And comes.

This not withstanding, thou wentst on,
And didst allow us all our noise:

Nay, thou hast made a sigh and groan
        Thy joys.

Not that thou hast not still above
Much better tunes, than groans can make;
But that these country airs thy love
        Did take.

Wherefore I cry, and cry again;
And in no quiet canst thou be,
Till I a thankful heart obtain
        Of thee:

Not thankful, when it pleaseth me;
As if thy blessings had spare days:
But such a heart, whose pulse may be
        Thy praise.

Love

Love bade me welcome: yet my soul drew back,
        Guilty of dust and sin.
But quick-ey'd Love, observing me grow slack
        From my first entrance in,
Drew nearer to me, sweetly questioning,
        If I lack'd anything.

A guest, I answer'd, worthy to be here:
        Love said, You shall be he.
I the unkind, ungrateful? Ah my dear,
        I cannot look on thee.
Love took my hand, and smiling did reply,
        Who made the eyes but I?

Truth Lord, but I have marr'd them: let my shame
        Go where it doth deserve.
And know you not, says Love, who bore the blame?
        My dear, then I will serve.

You must sit down, says Love, and taste my meat:
    So I did sit and eat.

The Call

Come, my Way, my Truth, my Life:
Such a Way, as gives us breath:
Such a Truth, as ends all strife:
And such a Life, as killeth death.

Come, my Light, my Feast, my Strength:
Such a Light, as shows a feast:
Such a Feast, as mends in length:
Such a Strength, as makes his guest.

Come, my Joy, my Love, my Heart:
Such a Joy, as none can move:
Such a Love, as none can part:
Such a Heart, as joys in love.

Spiritual Conflict

Sin

Lord, with what care hast thou begirt us round!
    Parents first season us: then schoolmasters
    Deliver us to laws; they send us bound
To rules of reason, holy messengers,
Pulpits and Sundays, sorrow dogging sin,
    Afflictions sorted, anguish of all sizes,
    Fine nets and stratagems to catch us in,
Bibles laid open, millions of surprises,
Blessings beforehand, ties of gratefulness,

The sound of glory ringing in our ears:
Without, our shame; within, our consciences;
Angels and grace, eternal hopes and fears.
Yet all these fences and their whole array
One cunning bosom-sin blows quite away.

The Collar

I struck the board, and cried, No more.
        I will abroad.
What? shall I ever sigh and pine?
My lines and life are free; free as the road,
    Loose as the wind, as large as store.
        Shall I be still in suit?
    Have I no harvest but a thorn
    To let me blood, and not restore
What I have lost with cordial fruit?
        Sure there was wine
    Before my sighs did dry it: there was corn
    Before my tears did drown it.
    Is the year only lost to me?
        Have I no bays to crown it?
No flowers, no garlands gay? all blasted?
        All wasted?
    Not so, my heart: but there is fruit,
        And thou hast hands.
    Recover all thy sigh-blown age
On double pleasures: leave thy cold dispute
Of what is fit, and not. Forsake thy cage,
        Thy rope of sands,
Which petty thoughts have made, and made to thee
    Good cable, to enforce and draw,
        And be thy law,
    While thou didst wink and wouldst not see.
        Away; take heed:
        I will abroad.
Call in thy death's head there: tie up thy fears.
        He that forbears

42

To suit and serve his need,
      Deserves his load.
But as I rav'd and grew more fierce and wild
      At every word,
Me thoughts I heard one calling, *Child:*
      And I replied, *My Lord*.

The Agony

      Philosophers have measur'd mountains,
Fathom'd the depths of seas, of states, and kings,
Walk'd with a staff to heav'n, and traced fountains:
      But there are two vast, spacious things,
The which to measure it doth more behove:
Yet few there are that sound them; Sin and Love.

      Who would know Sin, let him repair
Unto Mount Olivet; there shall he see
A man so wrung with pains, that all his hair,
      His skin, his garments bloody be.
Sin is that press and vice, which forceth pain
To hunt his cruel food through ev'ry vein.

      Who knows not Love, let him assay
And taste that juice, which on the cross a pike
Did set again abroach; then let him say
      If ever he did taste the like.
Love is that liquour sweet and most divine,
Which my God feels as blood; but I, as wine.

The Temper

How should I praise thee, Lord! how should my rhymes
      Gladly engrave thy love in steel,
      If what my soul doth feel sometimes,
            My soul might ever feel!

Although there were some forty heav'ns, or more,
   Sometimes I peer above them all;
   Sometimes I hardly reach a score,
     Sometimes to hell I fall.

Oh rack me not to such a vast extent;
   Those distances belong to thee:
   The world's too little for thy tent,
     A grave too big for me.

Wilt thou meet arms with man, that thou dost stretch
   A crumb of dust from heav'n to hell?
   Will great God measure with a wretch?
     Shall he thy stature spell?

Oh let me, when thy roof my soul hath hid,
   Oh let me roost and nestle there.
   Then of a sinner thou art rid,
     And I of hope and fear.

Yet take thy way; for sure thy way is best:
   Stretch or contract me thy poor debtor:
   This is but tuning of my breast,
     To make the music better.

Whether I fly with angels, fall with dust,
   Thy hands made both, and I am there:
   Thy power and love, my love and trust
     Make one place ev'rywhere.

Denial

   When my devotions could not pierce
      Thy silent ears;
Then was my heart broken, as was my verse:
     My breast was full of fears
      And disorder.

My bent thoughts, like a brittle bow,
　　　Did fly asunder:
Each took his way; some would to pleasures go,
　　Some to the wars and thunder
　　　Of alarms.

As good go anywhere, they say,
　　　As to benumb
Both knees and heart, in crying night and day,
　　Come, come, my God, Oh come,
　　　But no hearing.

Oh that thou shouldst give dust a tongue
　　　To cry to thee,
And then not hear it crying! all day long
　　My heart was in my knee,
　　　But no hearing.

Therefore my soul lay out of sight,
　　　Untun'd, unstrung:
My feeble spirit, unable to look right,
　　Like a nipp'd blossom, hung
　　　Discontented.

Oh cheer and tune my heartless breast,
　　　Defer no time;
That so thy favours granting my request,
　　They and my mind may chime,
　　　And mend my rhyme.

Bitter-Sweet

Ah my dear angry Lord,
Since thou dost love, yet strike;
Cast down, yet help afford;
Sure I will do the like.
I will complain, yet praise;
I will bewail, approve:

And all my sour-sweet days
I will lament, and love.

The Flower

How fresh, Oh Lord, how sweet and clean
Are thy returns! ev'n as the flowers in spring;
    To which, besides their own demean;
The late-past frosts tributes of pleasure bring.
        Grief melts away
        Like snow in May,
    As if there were no such cold thing.

Who would have thought my shrivell'd heart
Could have recover'd greenness? It was gone
    Quite underground; as flowers depart
To see their mother-root, when they have blown;
        Where they together
        All the hard weather,
    Dead to the world, keep house unknown.

These are thy wonders, Lord of power,
Killing and quick'ning, bringing down to hell
    And up to heaven in an hour;
Making a chiming of a passing-bell.
        We say amiss,
        This or that is:
    Thy word is all, if we could spell.

Oh that I once past changing were,
Fast in thy Paradise, where no flower can wither!
    Many a spring I shoot up fair,
Off'ring at heav'n, growing and groaning thither:
        Nor doth my flower
        Want a spring shower,
    My sins and I joining together:

But while I grow in a straight line,

Still upwards bent, as if heav'n were mine own,
    Thy anger comes, and I decline:
What frost to that? what pole is not the zone,
        Where all things burn,
        When thou dost turn,
    And the least frown of thine is shown?

    And now in age I bud again,
After so many deaths I live and write;
    I once more smell the dew and rain
And relish versing: Oh my only light,
        It cannot be
        That I am he
    On whom thy tempests fell all night.

    These are thy wonders, Lord of love,
To make us see we are but flowers that glide:
    Which when we once can find and prove,
Thou hast a garden for us, where to bide.
        Who would be more,
        Swelling through store,
    Forfeit their Paradise by their pride.

The Water Course

Thou who dost dwell and linger here below,
Since the condition of this world is frail,
Where of all plants afflictions soonest grow;
If troubles overtake thee, do not wail:

                                        Life.
    For who can look for less, that loveth
                                        Strife.

But rather turn the pipe, and water's course
To serve thy sins, and furnish thee with store
Of sov'reign tears, spring from true remorse:
That so in pureness thou mayest him adore,

                                        Salvation.
    Who gives to man, as he sees fit
                                        Damation.

THE COUNTRY PARSON

The Author to the Reader

BEING desirous (through the mercy of God) to please him, for whom I am, and live, and who giveth me my desires and performances; and considering with myself, that the way to please him, is to feed my flock diligently and faithfully, since our Saviour hath made that the argument of a pastor's love, I have resolved to set down the form and character of a true pastor, that I may have a mark to aim at: which also I will set as high as I can, since he shoots higher that threatens the moon, than he that aims at a tree. Not that I think, if a man do not all which is here expressed, he presently sins, and displeases God, but that it is a good strife to go as far as we can in pleasing of him, who hath done so much for us. The Lord prosper the intention to myself, and others, who may not despise my poor labours, but add to those points which I have observed, until the book grow to a complete pastoral.

GEO. HERBERT
1632

Of a Pastor

A Pastor is the deputy of Christ for the reducing of man to the obedience of God. This definition is evident, and contains the direct steps of pastoral duty and authority. For first, man fell from God by disobedience. Secondly, Christ is the glorious instrument of God for the revoking of man. Thirdly, Christ being not to continue on earth, but after he had fulfilled the work of reconciliation, to be received up into heaven, he constituted deputies in his place, and these are priests.

Out of this charter of the priesthood may be plainly gathered both the dignity thereof, and the duty: the dignity, in that a priest may do that which Christ did, and by his authority, and as his vice-regent. The duty, in that a priest is to do that which Christ did, and after his manner, both for doctrine and life.

The Parson's Life

The Country Parson is exceedingly exact in his life, being holy, just, prudent, temperate, bold, grave, in all his ways. And because the two highest points of life, wherein a Christian is most seen, are patience, and mortification; patience in regard of afflictions, mortification in regard of lusts and affections, and the stupefying and deading of all the clamorous powers of the soul, therefore he hath thoroughly studied these, that he may be an absolute master and commander of himself, for all the purposes which God hath ordained him.

Yet in these points he labours most in those things which are most apt to scandalize his parish. And first, because country people live hardly, and therefore as feeling their own sweat, and consequently knowing the price of money, are offended with any, who by hard usage increase their travel, the country parson is very circumspect in avoiding all covetousness, neither being greedy to get, nor niggardly to keep, nor troubled to lose any worldly wealth; but in all his words and actions slighting, and disesteeming it, even to a wondering, that the world should so much value wealth, which in the day of wrath hath not one dram of comfort for us. Secondly, because luxury is a very visible sin, the parson is very careful to avoid all kinds thereof, but especially that of drinking, because it is the most popular vice.

Thirdly, because country people (as indeed all honest

men) do much esteem their word, it being the life of buying and selling, and dealing in the world; therefore the parson is very strict in keeping his word, though it be to his own hindrance, as knowing that if he be not so, he will quickly be discovered and disregarded: neither will they believe him in the pulpit, whom they cannot trust in his conversation. As for oaths, and apparel, the disorders thereof are also very manifest. The parson's yea is yea, and nay, nay: and his apparel plain, but reverend, and clean, without spots, or dust, or smell; the purity of his mind breaking out, and dilating itself even to his body, clothes and habitation.

The Parson's Knowledge

The Country Parson is full of all knowledge. They say, it is an ill mason that refuseth any stone: and there is no knowledge, but, in a skilful hand, serves either positively as it is, or else to illustrate some other knowledge. He condescends even to the knowledge of tillage, and pasturage, and makes great use of them in teaching, because people, by what they understand, are best led to what they understand not.

The chief and top of his knowledge consists in the Book of books, the storehouse, and magazine of life and comfort, the Holy Scriptures. There he sucks, and lives. In the Scriptures he finds four things: precepts for life, doctrines for knowledge, examples for illustration, and promises for comfort: these he hath digested severally.

But for the understanding of these; the means he useth are first, a holy life. The second means is prayer, which if it be necessary even in temporal things, how much more in things of another world, where the well is deep, and we have nothing of ourselves to draw with? Wherefore he ever begins the reading of the Scripture with some short inward ejaculation, as, *Lord, open mine eyes, that I may see the wondrous things of thy law*, etc. The third means is a diligent collation of Scripture with Scripture.

For all truth being consonant to itself, and all being penned by one and the self-same Spirit, it cannot be, but that an industrious, and judicious comparing of place with place, must be a singular help for the right understanding of the Scriptures. The fourth means are commentators and fathers, who have handled the places controverted, which the parson by no means refuseth.

As he doth not so study others, as to neglect the grace of God in himself, and what the Holy Spirit teacheth him; so doth he assure himself, that God in all ages hath his servants, to whom he hath revealed his truth, as well as to him; and that as one country doth not bear all things, that there may be a commerce; so neither hath God opened, or will open all to one, that there may be a traffic in knowledge between the servants of God, for the planting both of love, and humility. Wherefore he hath one commentary at least upon every book of Scripture, and ploughing with this, and his own meditations, he enters into the secrets of God treasured in the Holy Scriptures.

The Parson's Accessory Knowledge

The Country Parson hath read the fathers also, and the schoolmen, and the later writers, or a good proportion of all, out of all which he hath compiled a book, and body of divinity, which is the storehouse of his sermons, and which he preacheth all his life; but diversely clothed, illustrated, and enlarged. For though the world is full of such composures, yet every man's own is fittest, readiest, and most savoury to him. Besides, this being to be done in his younger and preparatory times, it is an honest joy ever to look upon his well-spent hours.

The Parson Preaching

The Country Parson preacheth constantly, the pulpit is his joy and his throne. When he preacheth, he procures attention by all possible art, both by earnestness of speech, it being natural to men to think, that where is much earnestness, there is something worth hearing: and by a diligent cast of his eye upon his auditors, with letting them know he observes who marks, and who not; and with particularizing of his speech now to the younger sort, then to the elder, now to the poor, and now to the rich. This is for you, and this is for you; for particulars ever touch, and awake more than generals. Herein also he serves himself of the judgments of God, as of those of ancient times, so especially of the late ones; and those most, which are nearest to his parish; for people are very attentive at such discourses, and think it behoves them to be so, when God is so near them, and even over their heads.

Sometimes he tells them stories, and sayings of others, according as his text invites them; for them also men heed, and remember better than exhortations; which though earnest, yet often die with the sermon, especially with country people; which are thick, and heavy, and hard to raise to a point of zeal, and fervency, and need a mountain of fire to kindle them; but stories and sayings they will well remember. He often tells them that sermons are dangerous things, that none goes out of church as he came in, but either better or worse; that none is careless before his judge, and that the Word of God shall judge us. By these and other means the parson procures attention; but the character of his sermon is holiness. He is not witty, or learned, or eloquent, but holy.

The parson's method in handling of a text, consists of two parts: first, a plain and evident declaration of the meaning of the text: and secondly, some choice observations drawn out of the whole text, as it lies entire, and unbroken in the Scripture itself. This he thinks natural, and sweet, and grave.

The parson exceeds not an hour in preaching, because all ages have thought that a competency, and he that profits not in that time, will less afterwards, the same affection which made him not to profit before, making him then weary, and so he grows from not relishing, to loathing.

The Parson on Sundays

The Country Parson, as soon as he awakes on Sunday morning, presently falls to work, and seems to himself so as a market-man is, when the market-day comes, or a shopkeeper, when customers use to come in. His thoughts are full of making the best of the day, and contriving it to his best gains. To this end, besides his ordinary prayers, he makes a peculiar one for a blessing on the exercises of the day. That nothing befall him unworthy of that Majesty, before which he is to present himself, but that all may be done with reverence to His glory, and with edification to his flock, humbly beseeching his Master, that how or whenever he punish him, it be not in his ministry. Then he turns to request for his people, that the Lord would be pleased to sanctify them all, that they may come with holy hearts, and awful minds into the congregation, and that the good God would pardon all those who come with less prepared hearts, than they ought. This done, he sets himself to the consideration of the duties of the day, and if there be any extraordinary addition to the customary exercises.

Afterwards when the hour calls, with his family attending him, he goes to church, at his first entrance humbly adoring and worshipping the invisible majesty and presence of Almighty God, and blessing the people, either openly, or to himself. Then having read divine service twice fully, and preached in the morning, and catechized in the afternoon, he thinks he hath in some measure, according to poor and frail man, discharged the public duties of the congregation. The rest of the day he spends either in reconciling neighbours that are at variance, or in visiting the sick, or in exhortations to some of his flock by themselves, whom his sermons cannot, or do not reach.

At night he thinks it a very fit time; both suitable to the joy of the day, and without hindrance to public duties, either to entertain some of his neighbours, or to be entertained of them, where he takes occasion to discourse of such things as are both profitable and pleasant. As he opened the day with prayer, so he closeth it, humbly beseeching the Almighty to pardon and accept our poor services, and to improve them, that we may grow therein, and that our feet may be like unto hinds' feet, ever climbing up higher and higher unto him.

The Parson in his House

The Parson is very exact in the governing of his house; making it a copy and model for his parish. He knows the temper and pulse of every person in his house, and accordingly either meets with their vices, or advanceth their virtues.

His wife is either religious, or night and day he is winning her to it. Instead of the qualities of the world, he requires only three of her: first, a training up of her children and maids in the fear of God, with prayers, and catechizing, and all religious duties. Secondly, a curing and healing of all wounds and sores with her own hands; which skill either she brought with her, or he takes care she shall learn it of some religious neighbour. Thirdly, a providing for her family in such sort, as that neither they want a competent sustentation, nor her husband be brought into debt.

His children he first makes Christians, and then

commonwealth's men; the one he owes to his heavenly country, the other to his earthly, having no title to either, except he do good in both. Therefore having seasoned them with all piety, not only of words in praying, and reading; but in actions, in visiting other sick children, and tending their wounds, and sending his charity by them to the poor, and sometimes giving them a little money to do it of themselves, that they get a delight in it, and enter favour with God, who weighs even children's actions.

His servants are all religious, and were it not his duty to have them so, it were his profit, for none are so well served, as by religious servants, both because they do their best, and because what they do, is blessed and prospers. After religion, he teacheth them, that three things make a complete servant, truth, and diligence, and neatness, or cleanliness. Those that can read, are allowed times for it, and those that cannot, are taught; for all in his house are either teachers or learners, or both, so that his family is a school of religion, and they all account, that to teach the ignorant is the greatest alms.

He suffers not a lie or equivocation by any means in his house, but counts it the art and secret of governing, to preserve a directness, and open plainness in all things; so that all his house knows, that there is no help for a fault done, but confession. He himself, or his wife, takes account of sermons, and how every one profits, comparing this year with the last: and besides the common prayers of the family, he straightly requires of all to pray by themselves before they sleep at night, and stir out in the morning, and knows what prayers they say, and till they have learned them, makes them kneel by him.

The furniture of his house is very plain, but clean, whole, and sweet, as sweet as his garden can make; for he hath no money for such things, charity being his only perfume, which deserves cost when he can spare it.

His fare is plain, and common, but wholesome, what

he hath, is little, but very good; it consisteth most of mutton, beef, and veal, if he adds any thing for a great day, or a stranger, his garden or orchard supplies it, or his barn.

The Parson in his house observes fasting days: and particularly, as Sunday is his day of joy, so Friday is his day of humiliation, which he celebrates not only with abstinence of diet, but also of company, recreation, and all outward contentments; and besides, with confession of sins, and all acts of mortification.

The Parson's Courtesy

The Country Parson owing a debt of charity to the poor, and of courtesy to his other parishioners, he so distinguisheth, that he keeps his money for the poor, and table for those that are above alms. Not but that the poor are welcome also to his table, whom he sometimes purposely takes home with him, setting them close by him, and carving for them, both for his own humility and their comfort, who are much cheered with such friendliness. But since both is to be done, the better sort invited, and meaner relieved, he chooseth to give the poor money, which they can better employ to their own advantage, and suitably to their needs, than so much given in meat at dinner.

Having then invited some of his parish, he taketh his times to do the like to the rest; so that in the compass of the year, he hath them all with him, because country people are very observant of such things, and will not be persuaded, but being not invited, they are hated. Which persuasion the parson by all means avoids, knowing that where there are such conceits, there is no room for his doctrine to enter. Yet doth he oftenest invite those whom he sees take best courses, that so both they may be encouraged to persevere, and others spurred to do well, that they may enjoy the like courtesy.

For though he desire, that all should live well and

virtuously, not for any reward of his, but for virtue's sake; yet that will not be so: and therefore as God, although we should love him only for his own sake, yet out of his infinite pity hath set forth heaven for a reward to draw men to piety, and is content, if at least so, they will become good. So the Country Parson, who is a diligent observer and tracker of God's ways, sets up as many encouragements to goodness as he can, both in honour and profit, and fame; that he may, if not the best way, yet any way, make his parish good.

The Parson's Charity

The Country Parson is full of charity; it is his predominant element. When he riseth in the morning, he bethinketh himself what good deeds he can do that day, and presently doth them; counting that day lost, wherein he hath not exercised his charity.

He first considers his own parish, and takes care, that there be not a beggar, or idle person in his parish, but that all be in a competent way of getting their living. This he effects either by bounty, or persuasion, or by authority, making use of that excellent statute, which binds all parishes to maintain their own.

Besides this general provision, he hath other times of opening his hand; as at great festivals and communions; not suffering any that day he receives, to want a good meal suiting to the joy of the occasion. But specially, at hard times, and dearths, he even parts his living, and life among them, giving some corn outright, and selling other at under rates; and when his own stock serve not, working those that are able to the same charity, still pressing it in the pulpit and out of the pulpit, and never leaving them till he obtain his desire. Yet in all his charity, he distinguisheth, giving them most, who live best, and take most pains, and are most charged: so is his charity in effect a sermon.

Whenever he gives anything, and sees them labour in

thanking of him, he exacts of them to let him alone, and say rather, God be praised, God be glorified; so that the thanks may go the right way, and thither only, where they are due. For other givings are lay, and secular, but this is to give like a priest.

The Parson's Church

The Country Parson hath a special care of his church, that all things there be decent, and befitting his name by which it is called. Therefore first he takes order, that all things be in good repair; as walls plastered, windows glazed, floor paved, seats whole, firm, and uniform, especially that the pulpit, and desk, and communion table, and font be as they ought, for those great duties that are performed in them. Secondly, that the church be swept, and kept clean without dust, or cobwebs, and at great festivals strewed, and stuck with boughs, and perfumed with incense. Thirdly, that there be fit and proper texts of Scripture everywhere painted, and that all the painting be grave, and reverend, not with light colours and foolish antics. Fourthly, that all the books appointed by authority be there, and those not torn, or fouled, but whole and clean, and well bound; and that there be a fitting, and sightly communion cloth of fine linen, with an handsome, and seemly carpet of good and costly stuff, or cloth, and all kept sweet and clean, in a strong and decent chest, with a chalice, and cover, and a stoop or flagon; and a basin for alms and offerings; besides which, he hath a poor man's box conveniently seated, to receive the charity of well-minded people, and to lay up treasure for the sick and needy.

The Parson in Circuit

The Country Parson upon the afternoons in the week-days, takes occasion sometimes to visit in person, now one quarter of his parish, now another. For there he shall find his flock most naturally as they are, wallowing in the midst of their affairs: whereas on Sunday it is easy for them to compose themselves to order, which they put on as their holy-day clothes, and come to church in frame, but commonly the next day put them off.

When he comes to any house, first he blesseth it, and then as he finds the persons of the house employed, so he forms his discourse. Those that he finds religiously employed, he both commends them much and furthers them when he is gone, in their employment; as if he finds them reading, he furnisheth them with good books; if curing poor people, he supplies them with receipts, and instructs them further in that skill, showing them how acceptable such works are to God.

Those that he finds busy in the works of their calling, he commendeth them also: for it is a good and just thing for every one to do their own business. But then he admonisheth them of two things: first that they dive not too deep into worldly affairs, plunging themselves over head and ears into carking and caring; but that they so labour, as neither to labour anxiously, nor distrustfully, nor profanely. Then they labour anxiously, when they overdo it, to the loss of their quiet, and health: then distrustfully, when they doubt God's providence, thinking that their own labour is the cause of their thriving, as if it were in their own hands to thrive, or not to thrive. Secondly, he adviseth them so to labour for wealth, and maintenance as that they make not that the end of their labour, but that they may have wherewithal to serve God the better, and to do good deeds.

Those that the parson finds idle, or ill-employed, he chides not at first, for that were neither civil, nor profitable; but always in the close, before he departs from them.

Besides these occasional discourses, the parson questions what order is kept in the house, as about prayers morning, and evening on their knees, reading of Scripture, catechizing, singing of psalms at their work, and

on holy days; who can read, and who not; and sometimes
he hears the children read himself, and blesseth, encour-
aging also the servants to learn to read, and offering to
have them taught on holidays by his servants. If the
parson were ashamed of particularizing in these things,
he were not fit to be a parson; but he holds the rule,
that nothing is little in God's service; if it once have the
honour of that name, it grows great instantly. Wherefore
neither disdaineth he to enter into the poorest cottage,
though he even creep into it, and though it smell never
so loathesomely. For both God is there also, and those
for whom God died.

These are the parson's general aims in his circuit; but
with these he mingles other discourses for conversation
sake, and to make his higher purposes slip the more
easily.

The Parson a Father

The Country Parson is not only a father to his flock,
but also professeth himself thoroughly of the opinion,
carrying it about with him as fully as if he had begot
his whole parish. And of this he makes great use. For
by this means when any sins, he hateth him not as an
officer, but pities him as a father: and even in those
wrongs which either in tithing, or otherwise are done to
his own person, he considers the offender as a child, and
forgives, so he may have any sign of amendment; so
also when after many admonitions, any continue to be
refractory, yet he gives him not over, but is long before
he proceed to disinheriting, or perhaps never goes so far;
knowing that some are called at the eleventh hour, and
therefore he still expects, and waits, lest he should deter-
mine God's hour of coming; which as he cannot,
touching the last day, so neither touching the inter-
mediate days of conversion.

The Parson in Journey

The Country Parson, when a just occasion calleth him out of his parish (which he diligently, and strictly weigheth, his parish being all his joy, and thought) leaveth not his ministry behind him; but is himself wherever he is. Therefore those he meets on the way he blesseth audibly, and with those he overtakes or that overtake him, he begins good discourses, such as may edify him, interposing sometimes some short and honest refreshments, which may make his discourses more welcome, and less tedious.

And when he comes to his inn, he refuseth not to join, that he may enlarge the glory of God to the company he is in, by a due blessing of God for their safe arrival, and saying grace at meat, and at going to bed by giving the host notice, that he will have prayers in the hall, wishing him to inform his guests thereof, that if any be willing to partake, they may resort thither. The like he doth in the morning, using pleasantly the outlandish proverb, that *prayers and provender never hinder journeys.*

The Parson in Reference

If God have sent any calamity either by fire or famine, to any neighbouring parish, then he expects no brief; but taking his parish together the next Sunday, or holyday, and exposing to them the uncertainty of human affairs, none knowing whose turn may be next, and then when he hath affrighted them with this, exposing the obligation of charity, and neighbourhood, he first gives himself liberally, and then incites them to give; making together a sum either to be sent, or, which were more comfortable, all together choosing some fit day to carry it themselves, and cheer the afflicted.

The Parson in Sacraments

The Country Parson being to administer the sacraments, is at a stand with himself, how or what behaviour to assume for so holy things. Especially at communion times he is in a great confusion, as being not only to receive God, but to break and administer him. Neither finds he any issue in this, but to throw himself down at the throne of grace, saying, Lord, thou knowest what thou didst, when thou appointedst it to be done thus; therefore do thou fulfil what thou didst appoint; for thou art not only the feast, but the way to it.

At baptism, being himself in white, he requires the presence of all, and baptizeth not willingly, but on Sundays, or great days. He admits no vain or idle names, but such as are usual and accustomed. He says that prayer with great devotion, where God is thanked for calling us to the knowledge of his grace, baptism being a blessing, that the world hath not the like. He willingly and cheerfully crosseth the child, and thinketh the ceremony not only innocent, but reverend.

He instructeth the godfathers, and godmothers, that it is no complemental or light thing to sustain that place, but a great honour, and no less burden, as being done both in the presence of God, and his saints, and by way of undertaking for a Christian soul. He adviseth all to call to mind their baptism often, for if wise men have thought it the best way of preserving a state to reduce it to its principles by which it grew great; certainly it is the safest course for Christians also to meditate on their baptism often (being the first step into their great and glorious calling) and upon what terms, and with what vows they were baptized.

At the times of the Holy Communion, he first takes order with the churchwardens, that the elements be of the best, not cheap, or coarse, much less ill-tasted, or unwholesome. Secondly, he considers and looks into the ignorance, or carelessness of his flock, and accordingly applies himself with catechizings, and lively exhortations, not on the Sunday of the communion only (for then it is too late) but the Sunday, or Sundays before the communion, or on the eves of all those days.

If there be any, who having not received yet, is to enter into this great work, he takes the more pains with them, that he may lay the foundation of future blessings.

For the manner of receiving, as the parson useth all reverence himself, so he administers to none but to the reverent. The feast indeed requires sitting, because it is a feast; but man's unpreparedness asks kneeling. He that comes to the sacrament, hath the confidence of a guest, and he that kneels, confesseth himself an unworthy one, and therefore differs from other feasters: but he that sits, or lies, puts up to an apostle: contentiousness in a feast of charity is more scandal than any posture.

The Parson's Completeness

The Country Parson desires to be all to his parish, and not only a pastor, but a lawyer also, and a physician. Therefore he endures not that any of his flock should go to law; but in any controversy, that they should resort to him as their judge. To this end he hath gotten himself some insight in things ordinarily incident and controverted, by experience, and by reading some initiatory treatises in the law.

In judging he follows that, which is altogether right; so that if the poorest man of the parish detain but a pin unjustly from the richest, he absolutely restores it as a judge; but when he hath so done, then he assumes the parson, and exhorts to charity. Nevertheless, there may happen sometimes some cases wherein he chooseth to permit his parishioners rather to make use of the law than himself. But then he shows them how to go to law, even as brethren, and not as enemies.

Now as the parson is in law, so is he in sickness also: if there be any of his flock sick, he is their physician, or at least his wife, of whom instead of the qualities of the world, he asks no other, but to have the skill of healing a wound, or helping the sick. But if neither himself, nor his wife have the skill, and his means serve, he keeps some young practitioner in his house for the benefit of his parish, whom yet he exhorts not to exceed his bounds; but in difficult cases to call in help. If all fail, he keeps good correspondence with some neighbour physician, and entertains him for the cure of his parish. Yet it is easy for any scholar to attain to such a measure of physic, as may be of much use to him both for himself, and others. This is done by seeing one anatomy, reading one book of physic, having one herbal by him.

Now both the reading, and the knowing of herbs, may be done at such times as they may be a help and a recreation to more divine studies, nature serving grace both in the comfort of diversion, and the benefit of application when need requires. As also, by way of illustration, our Saviour made plants and seeds to teach the people: for he was the true householder, who bringeth out of his treasure things new and old; the old things of philosophy, and the new of grace; and maketh the one serve the other. And I conceive, our Saviour did this for three reasons: first, that by familiar things he might make his doctrine slip the more easily into the hearts even of the meanest. Secondly, that labouring people (whom he chiefly considered) might have everywhere monuments of his doctrine, remembering in gardens, his mustard-seed, and lilies; in the field, his seed-corn, and tares; and so not be drowned altogether in the works of their vocation, but sometimes lift up their minds to better things, even in the midst of their pains. Thirdly, that he might set a copy for parsons.

In the knowledge of simples, wherein the manifold wisdom of God is wonderfully to be seen, one thing would be carefully observed; which is, to know what herbs may be used instead of drugs of the same nature, and to make the garden the shop: for home-bred medicines are both more easy for the parson's purse, and more familiar for all men's bodies. Accordingly for salves, his wife seeks not the city, but prefers her garden and fields, before all outlandish gums. And surely hyssop, valerian, mercury, adder's tongue, yerrow, melilot, and St. John's-wort made into a salve; and elder, camomile, mallows, comphrey and smallage made into a poultice, have done great and rare cures. In curing of any, the parson and his family use to promise prayers, for this is to cure like a parson, this raiseth the action from the shop, to the church.

The Parson in Mirth

The Country Parson is generally sad, because he knows nothing but the cross of Christ, his mind being defixed on it with those nails wherewith his master was; or if he have any leisure to look off from thence he meets continually with two most sad spectacles; sin and misery; God dishonoured every day, and man afflicted.

Nevertheless, he sometimes refresheth himself, as knowing that nature will not bear everlasting droopings, and that pleasantness of disposition is a great key to do good; not only because all men shun the company of perpetual severity, but also for that when they are in company, instructions seasoned with pleasantness, both enter sooner, and root deeper. Wherefore he condescends to human frailties both in himself and others; and intermingles some mirth in his discourses occasionally, according to the pulse of the hearer.

The Parson's Consideration of Providence

The Country Parson considering the great aptness country people have, to think that all things come by a kind of natural course; and that if they sow and soil their grounds, they must have corn; if they keep and fodder well their cattle, they must have milk, and calves; labours to reduce them to see God's hand in all things, and to believe, that things are not set in such an inevitable order, but that God often changeth it according as he sees fit, either for reward or punishment. To this end he represents to his flock, that God hath and exerciseth a threefold power in every thing which conerns man. The first is a sustaining power; the second, a governing power; the third, a spiritual power.

By his sustaining power he preserves and actuates every thing in his being; so that corn doth not grow by any other virtue, than by that which he continually supplies, as the corn needs it; without which supply the corn would instantly dry up, as a river would, if the fountain were stopped.

By God's governing power he preserves and orders the references of things one to the other, so that though the corn do grow, and be preserved in that act by his sustaining power, yet if he suit not other things to the growth, as seasons, and weather, and other accidents, by his governing power, the fairest harvests come to nothing. And it is observable, that God delights to have men feel, and acknowledge, and reverence his power, and therefore he often overturns things, when they are thought past danger. That is his time of interposing. As when a merchant hath a ship come home after many a storm, which it hath escaped, he destroys it sometimes in the very haven; or if the goods be housed, a fire hath broken forth, and suddenly consumed them.

Now this he doth, that men should perpetuate, and not break off their acts of dependence, how fair soever the opportunities present themselves. So that if a farmer should depend upon God all the year, and being ready to put hand to sickle, shall then secure himself, and think all cock-sure; then God sends such weather, as lays the corn, and destroys it: or if he depend on God further, even till he imbarn his corn, and then think all sure; God sends a fire and consumes all that he hath: for that he ought not to break off, but to continue his dependence on God, not only before the corn is inned, but after also; and, indeed, to depend, and fear continually.

The third power is spiritual, by which God turns all outward blessings to inward advantages. So that if a farmer hath both a fair harvest, and that also well inned, and imbarned, and continuing safe there; yet if God give him not the grace to use and utter this well, all his advantages are to his loss. And it is observable in this, how God's goodness strives with man's refractoriness; man would sit down at this world, God bids him sell it, and purchase a better.

The Parson's Library

The Country Parson's library is a holy life: for besides the blessing that that brings upon it, there being a promise, that if the kingdom of God be first sought, all other things shall be added, even itself a sermon. For the temptations with which a good man is beset, and the ways which he used to overcome them, being told to another, whether in private conference, or in the church, are a sermon.

He that hath considered how to carry himself at table about his appetite, if he tell this to another, preacheth; and much more feelingly, and judiciously, than he writes his rules of temperance out of books. So that the parson having studied and mastered all his lusts and affections within, and the whole army of temptations without, hath ever so many sermons ready penned, as he hath victories.

The Parson's Dexterity in Applying of Remedies

The Country Parson knows, that there is a double state of a Christian, even in this life, the one military, the other peaceable. The military is, when we are assaulted with temptations either from within or from without. The peaceable is, when the devil for a time leaves us, as he did our Saviour, and the angels minister to us their own food, even joy, and peace, and comfort in the Holy

Ghost. Now the parson having a spiritual judgement, according as he discovers any of his flock to be in one or the other state, so he applies himself to them.

Those that he finds in the peaceable state, he adviseth to be very vigilant, and not to let go the reins as soon as the horse goes easy. Particularly, he counselleth them to two things: first, to take heed, lest their quiet betray them (as it is apt to do) to a coldness, and carelessness in their devotions, but to labour still to be as fervent in Christian duties, as they remember themselves were, when affliction did blow the coals. Secondly, not to take the full compass and liberty of their peace: not to eat of all the dishes at table, which even their present health otherwise admits; nor to store their house with all those furnitures which even their present plenty of wealth admits; nor when they are among them that are merry, to extend themselves to all that mirth, which the present occasion of wit, and company otherwise admits; but to put bounds and hoops to their joys: so will they last the longer, and when they depart, return the sooner.

Now in those that are tempted, whatsoever is unruly, falls upon two heads; either they think, that there is none that can or will look after things, but all goes by chance, or wit: or else, though there be a great Governor of all things, yet to them he is lost, as if they said, God doth forsake and persecute them, and there is none to deliver them.

If the parson suspect the first and find sparks of such thoughts now and then to break forth, then without opposing directly (for disputation is no cure for atheism) he scatters in his discourse arguments, taken from nature and grace.

But if he sees them nearer desperation, than atheism, not so much doubting a God, as that he is theirs; then he dives into the boundless ocean of God's love, and the unspeakable riches of his loving-kindness.

The Parson's Condescending

The Country Parson is a lover of old customs, if they be good and harmless; and the rather, because country people are much addicted to them, so that to favour them therein is to win their hearts, and to oppose them therein is to deject them. If there be any evil in the custom, that may be severed from the good, he pares the apple, and gives them the clean to feed on.

Particularly, he loves procession, and maintains it, because there are contained therein four manifest advantages: first, a blessing of God for the fruits of the field: secondly, justice in the preservation of bounds: thirdly, charity in loving walking, and neighbourly accompanying one another, with reconciling of differences at that time, if there be any: fourthly, relieving the poor by a liberal distribution and largess, which at that time is, or ought to be used. Wherefore he exacts of all to be present at the perambulation, and those that withdraw, and sever themselves from it, he mislikes, and reproves as uncharitable and unneighbourly; and if they will not reform, presents them. Nay, he is so far from condemning such assemblies, that he rather procures them to be often, as knowing that absence breeds strangeness, but presence love.

Now love is his business and aim; wherefore he likes well, that his parish at good times invite one another to their houses, and he urgeth them to it: and sometimes, where he knows there hath been or is a little difference, he takes one of the parties, and goes with him to the other, and all dine or sup together. There is much preaching in this friendliness.

Another old custom there is of saying, when light is brought in, God send us the light of heaven; and the parson likes this very well: neither is he afraid of praising, or praying to God at all times, but is rather glad of catching opportunities to do them. Light is a great blessing, and as great as food, for which we give thanks; and those that think this superstitious, neither know superstition nor themselves.

The Parson Blessing

The Country Parson wonders, that blessing the people is in so little use with his brethren: whereas he thinks it not only a grave, and reverend thing, but a beneficial also. Those who use it not; do so either out of niceness, because they like the salutations, and compliments, and forms of worldly language better; which conformity and fashionableness is so exceedingly unbefitting a minister, that it deserves reproof, not refutation: or else, because they think it empty and superfluous. But that which the Apostles used so diligently in their writings, nay, which our Saviour himself used, cannot be vain and superfluous.

Now blessing differs from prayer, in assurance, because it is not performed by way of request, but of confidence, and power, effectually applying God's favour to the blessed, by the interesting of that dignity wherewith God hath invested the priest, and engaging of God's own power and institution for a blessing.

OUTLANDISH PROVERBS

Life and Death

Life is half spent before we know what it is.

A cool mouth, and warm feet, live long.

He that lives in hope dances without music.

Let all live as they would die.

A fair death honours the whole life.

He begins to die, that quits his desires.

He that fears death lives not.

No church-yard is so handsome, that a man would desire straight to be buried there.

War is death's feast.

Death keeps no calender.

There is an hour wherein a man might be happy all his life, could he find it.

Between the business of life and the day of death, a space ought to be interposed.

Wisdom and Wit

Our own actions are our security, not others' judgments.

He that is not handsome at 20, nor strong at 30, nor rich at 40, nor wise at 50, will never be handsome, strong, rich or wise.

He that lies with the dogs, riseth with fleas.

No sooner is a temple built to God, but the devil builds a chapel hard by.

When all sins grow old, covetousness is young.

Everyone is weary, the poor in seeking, the rich in keeping, the good in learning.

He that will learn to pray, let him go to sea.

The itch of disputing is the scab of the church.

He that goes barefoot, must not plant thorns.

Better the feet slip than the tongue.

Though old and wise, yet still advise.

With customs we live well, but laws undo us.

Friends and Neighbours

Old wine, and an old friend, are good provisions.

When a friend asks, there is no tomorrow.

Love your neighbour, yet pull not down your hedge.

Three can hold their peace, if two be away.

Many things are lost for want of asking.

A mountain and a river are good neighbours.

The best mirror is an old friend.

He that's long a-giving, knows not how to give.

He that gives me small gifts would have me live.

It is good to have some friends both in heaven and hell.

All is well with him, who is beloved of his neighbours.

Many friends in general, one in special.

Marriage and Housekeeping

In choosing a wife, and buying a sword, we ought not to trust another.

Advise none to marry or to go to war.

He that tells his wife news is but newly married.

The more women look in their glass, the less they look to their house.

In a good house all is quickly ready.

A cheerful look makes a dish a feast.

He that hath a wife and children wants not business.

When children stand quiet, they have done some ill.

In the house of a fiddler, all fiddle.

The good mother says not, Will you? but gives.

He that wipes the child's nose, kisseth the mother's cheek.

The best smell is bread, the best savour is salt, the best love that of children.

Business and Labour

Who hath no haste in his business, mountains to him seem valleys.

Think of ease, but work on.

Would you know what money is, go borrow some.

He that makes a thing too fine, breaks it.

One grain fills not a sack, but helps his fellows.

Everyone thinks his sack the heaviest.

Speak not of my debts, unless you mean to pay them.

Two sparrows on one ear of corn make an ill agreement.

Working and making a fire doth discretion require.

Great fortune brings with it great misfortune.

Tithe, and be rich.

Where your will is ready, your feet are light.

Good and Evil

Keep good men company, and you shall be of the number.

Better to be blind, than to see ill.

Good is good, but better carries it.

Bear with evil, and expect good.

All things in their being are good for something.

Poverty is no sin.

He that lives ill, fear follows him.

Who would do ill ne'er wants occasion.

Good words quench more than a bucket of water.

Truth and oil are ever above.

He that hath no ill fortune is troubled with good.

Good words are worth much, and cost little.

Knowledge and Love

The heart's letter is read in the eyes.

Knowledge is folly, except grace guide it.

Love is the true price of love.

He that hath love in his breast, hath spurs in his sides.

There needs a long time to know the world's pulse.

Love makes one fit for any work.

He that lives well is learned enough.

Love and a cough cannot be hid.

A wise man needs not blush for changing his purpose.

Love rules his kingdom without a sword.

The wind in one's face makes one wise.

Love asks faith, and faith firmness.

THE FUTILITY OF WAR

I know that the name of war is splendid and glorious when the spirit is high and – unable to control itself – fiercely champs at triumphs and victories as though they were foaming bits, delighting to brandish the sword and gaze upon its point:

> Already the threatening trumpet-blast
> Hurts men's ears; already the bugles sound;
> Already the gleam of arms terrifies
> The fleeing horses and the faces of the horsemen.

But, since splendid things are generally brittle, ruining their brightness by their frailty, and since we are not speaking of private but of public advantage, we must confess that peace is to be preferred to war, for without peace all life is a storm and the whole world a desert. In peace, sons bury their fathers; in war, fathers their sons. In peace, the sick are made whole; in war, even the whole perish. In peace, there is safety in the fields; in war, not even within the city walls. In peace, the song of birds awakens us; in war, trumpets and drums. Peace opens up a new world; war destroys the old:

> Peace feeds the labourer well e'en amid rocks,
> But war e'en on the plain his labour mocks.

Within our own republic, the university, peace is essential for the Muses: without it we are nothing. How quickly the equipment of our art, our paper, pens and books, perish once the soldiers' conflagration has begun!

Of what use are your penknives if these very towers, these beautiful buildings, are to be destroyed with one blast of a canon? What have the Muses to do with such violence? The arts demand leisure: minds that are tranquil, serene and clear; groves in summer; thick cloaks in winter. Learning is a delicate and tender thing; like a soft flower, it withers away when touched by the rough hand of a soldier.

You who apply yourself to philosophy: while you are alleging that the linking of the body with the soul is a hindrance to contemplation, a soldier rushes into your study and sets you at liberty with his sword. You who explore the stars: while you are handling imaginary globes and heavens, an officer bursts in and thrusts you and your heavens down into the underworld. Such is what befell Archimedes when his dying body effaced the figures he had just inscribed in the sand. And so we must take care not to undervalue the peace that watches over the arts, acting as a midwife.

Know you not, I pray, the miseries of war? Consult the histories: there you have a safe way of learning, beyond the reach of weapons. Behold, slaughterings of every kind: mangled bodies, the mutilated image of God, a little span of life long enough for weeping, the burnings of cities, crashings, plunderings, violated virgins, women with child twice killed, little infants shedding more milk than blood; images, nay shadows of men, with hunger, cold, filth, vexed, crushed, disabled. How cruel is glory which is reared upon the necks of men, where it is doubtful whether he who achieves it, or he who suffers, is the more miserable!

Index of First Lines of Poems

Bibliography

The most recent biography of George Herbert is *A Life of George Herbert* by Amy Charles (Cornell University Press, 1977) which is based on careful and thorough research.

The Works of George Herbert, edited by F. E. Hutchinson (Oxford University Press, 1941), contains poetry, prose, proverbs, letters and orations in both English and Latin.

Herbert's major works are also contained in *George Herbert*, edited by John N. Wall, Jnr., in The Classics of Western Spiritualty Series (SPCK, 1981).

Two excellent personal collections of his poetry are *George Herbert*, selected by W. H. Auden (Penguin Books, 1973) and *A Choice of George Herbert's Verse*, selected by R. S. Thomas (Faber & Faber, 1986).

Acknowledgement

Our thanks to Horace Dammers who helped with translating the Latin oration.

Lament &Love

George Herbert's abiding vision was that the ordinary parish church could become a true Christian community — and as a country parson he put his vision into practice. He was also a passionate advocate of peace between nations, and as a young man sacrificed a promising career in politics by defying the King's military plans. Between his two careers as politician and parson he composed some of the best Christian poetry ever written, describing his own, often painful, spiritual journey.

This books contains an abridged version of his inspiring work 'The Country Parson', and also an extract of his great speech in the cause of peace. It has a selection of his poetry, arranged according to themes, such as the Christian festivals, so readers can readily choose poems for use in worship and meditation.

ISBN 0-551-01827-5

£1.99

LAMP

9 780551 018273

Babani Electronics Books

▶ High Power Audio Amplifier Construction

▶ **Audio and acoustics**

▶ **Circuits and projects**

▶ **Data and reference**

▶ **Music and MIDI**

▶ **Test equipment**

▶ **SW radio and communications**

▶ **R. A. Penfold**